IN THE FIELD BETWEEN US

IN THE FIELD

BETWEEN US

POEMS

Molly McCully Brown | Susannah Nevison

A Karen & Michael Braziller Book

PERSEA BOOKS | NEW YORK

Persea Books, Inc.
90 Broad Street
New York, New York 10004

Library of Congress Cataloging-in-Publication Data

Names: Brown, Molly McCully, 1991— author. | Nevison, Susannah, 1984– author.
Title: In the field between us : poems / [by Molly McCully Brown & Susannah Nevison]
Description: New York, New York : Persea Books, [2020] | Summary:
"In the Field Between Us is comprised of letters in verse between
Molly McCully Brown and Susannah Nevison, which ponders disability and the possibility of
belonging in the aftermath of lifelong medical intervention"—Provided by publisher.
Identifiers: LCCN 2019050186 | ISBN 9780892555147 (paperback)
Subjects: LCSH: People with disabilities—Poetry. | Disabilities—Poetry. |
Medical care—Poetry. | Loss (Psychology)—Poetry. | Belonging (Social psychology)—
Poetry. | Autobiographical poetry, American. | Epistolatory poetry.
Classification: LCC PS3602.R722354 I5 2020 | DDC 811/.6—dc23
LC record available at https://lccn.loc.gov/2019050186

Book design and composition by Rita Lascaro
Typeset in Minion
Manufactured in the United States of America.
Printed on acid-free paper.

ACKNOWLEDGMENTS

We'd like to extend our gratitude to the editors at the following publications, where many of these poems first appeared, sometimes in earlier forms: *Blackbird, Cincinnati Review, diode poetry journal,* The Eloquent Poem, *Indiana Review, Missouri Review,* the New York Times, the Phi Kappa Phi Forum, Tin House Magazine, and *Quarterly West.*

Poems from this collection were also reprinted at *isacoustic* and on the Academy of American Poets website.

Thanks to the Sewanee Writers' Conference, which offered us both scholarships in 2016 and helped facilitate the friendship that gave rise to this collaboration, and to the *Oxford American* magazine and the University of Utah, which provided us with individual fellowships that allowed us to devote time and energy to the project.

To our editor, Gabriel Fried: We're so grateful for your careful and intelligent eye and your faith in this book and the world we built together. Thank you for helping us make it real.

Particular gratitude to JP Grasser for turning his exacting intellect and attention to this manuscript. This book is so much smoother, subtler, and stronger for your edits.

Finally, to our families, we owe you everything: to Carrie and John Gregory, Jack and Nancy, Walker, Olivia, Kasandra and Orion, Vince, Laura, Lucia and Violet, Larry, Mary, Danny, Shaun and Helen, with love. And to David, with immeasurable gratitude: for reading, for listening, and for championing this book.

CONTENTS

AFTERMATH

DEAR M—

The dream where I'm legless
isn't a nightmare, and I'm not
afraid—there's light and a river
and everything is exactly
how I'd hoped. I'm not tethered
to the earth. I'm not tied down
by gravity, dragging my legs
along the bank gravel, not searching
for the softest patch of moss.
I'm not even tired, and though
I'm certain the dream
is an elegy, it sounds exactly like
a praise song. In the dream
my legs break free of me
and I watch them float away.
        The coffin in my chest
blows open in the wind,
and for once I think I know
what it's like to be without
all our dead and heavy things.

DEAR S—

I've said this all before
and anyway, you had
already been picked up,
held down, put under,
and refashioned;
you were already
dreaming your body
in some gravity-less
country, already calling
it a river, Mars. Let's go
back to wherever it is
we were made for first:
to water, or a rusted
windswept planet where
everything floats and women
are part horse or fox, knocked
off kilter and galloping left
to get where they were meant
to go. We'd miss it here eventually.
The boat that brought us, I believe
in it. But having found you
I am seeking out the channel
where we came from.
Sister, take my hand.

DEAR M—

There's a whole wild species
I don't know how to name, so instead
I say pain is an engine that stalls
the harder I push it or it's the stone
in my mouth I can't quite seem
to swallow. I'm not waiting
for someone else to tell me
what I'm missing. Numbness
is a quiet fire, a night in, a *call again*
tomorrow. I know sometimes
I go missing, dark, a lightless stretch
of road, so I spit the road out
as I go. What I'm missing
is the means to call again
tomorrow. What I'm missing is
a picture where the table's set
and all the versions of ourselves
sit down to eat, and when we open
our mouths, no roads or stones fall out.

Dear S—

Half the nights I still start awake as the bus
sputters past in the dark, or a coyote yowls
out where I was dreaming. Half the nights
I don't know my body when I wake to it,
and there's grief in the returning, remembering
pain, familiar as a fist I know. In the morning,
I wake and my body wears bruises I didn't make,
or don't remember making. Did it take off without me,
board a bus from this new city looking for home,
or glamour, or you? I wouldn't rule it out,
my body's always wished it were wilder.
      Maybe that's why there's always howling
in the distance, why we're always spitting
road and stones from somewhere else.
It's fall now, but this city doesn't know it.
In the morning, I call you and we compare mysteries:
*What do you make of it? Where do you think you went
last night?*

DEAR M—

Maybe it's a pronoun problem after all—
our bodies, you, and me, the lot of us
in search of ways to address each other,
when we can't ever fully turn around
inside this room. When we sleep, of course
we come unraveled: it's only fair. Awake
we're always pushing against another
kind of self, who pushes back,
or pulls us down, or makes us stay.
The kind who doesn't let us go too far,
who strokes our hair, keeps us tame.
When we sleep, I believe we
leave some selves behind. In the morning
they stare back at me across
the room, and though I look away,
they always plead with me:
tell us where we've been.

Dear S—

Today the doctor's office called to say he'd see me
in November, and take every photograph at once:
my knees, and hips, and back, to *see what's what.*
And I heard: *survey the damage; tell your fortune;*
reach right in; cast you out. And all my smaller
selves, they hunkered down like children,
tender in their fear, swore that they'd file down
their claws and fall in line, or let me loose
if that was what I wanted. Begged me
to keep them a secret, not to hold them
out there in the light. Years ago they spent
a long time in the theater: fumbling their blocking,
being stretched and prodded, asked to pose,
stitched together, rent apart. There are so many star
charts made in their image, so many maps
of how they move. But then there was this mess
of wild, unwatched years. My hair grew long,
my selves grew wedded to their unseen galaxy.
They want no cartograph, no telescope;
they want neither to know or to be known.
I have been asking for an answer, a relief
map. I have begged to be found out. Now
some maker readies the camera, readies
the compass, readies the knife, and all of me
rallies to pull the curtains closed, to cover my face.

Dear M—

I've wanted to be lost,
to wander in the forest
until all the trees refuse to give
me up. I've wanted to give up,
to call the doctor's bluff,
to say *here's no place to ground a fence,*
or *you can't corral what's good
and gone.* I've turned off all the lights,
closed every door, but the littler
selves come tumbling out no matter
what I do: they tug at the hem
of my dress, until I stop and say
their names. It's their favorite game,
making me trot them out in public
or at a party, like a gaudy Mardi Gras
parade. I say we give them
what they want. I say we dress them up
for one last show, doll them up
before we send them down
the road. We're all they know.
There are so many places left
for us to find, so many trees, a hundred
different ways to wander off.
So many different ways we might get lost.

Dear S—

I keep a lot of lanterns in the house
for the ways we might one day be able
to get lost, a lot of matches so my smaller
selves can light their way along the road.
They get distracted, drop them lit, a pasture
burns: tobacco, strawberries, our skin
comes right off with the plaster.
They seem surprised, sometimes, by all
the damage, other times they're just in love
with how the light takes over for awhile. S,
you're right, we're all they know. I send them
up the road, they trail a blaze right home
to climb back down the throat they came from,
hungry, tired from the show, and ill-equipped
to make it on their own. Who'd have
thought it, that anybody's country
was in our bones?

Dear M—

And then there's this other species
of grief I've stopped trying to name,
that pulls me to my knees,
that tempts me to look
over my shoulder at what
I could have done, or didn't do.
I can't give it a name the way
I couldn't name my unborn child,
because I don't want to look
into that same dark room where
I said *I won't be your mother,* where the girl
I was has already read *the forgetting is so long*
but can't possibly know how sharp
some memories become, armed
against tenderness or sleep.
I still carry a bloodmap
for a lost country, somewhere
between my body and a boy I loved
but also couldn't keep.   I'm afraid to touch
so many things because they'll disappear.
At night I turn toward the face
of the man I love, and dream of the space
between our bodies, his and mine,
where the forgetting cuts a road
that's long and wild, and I dream
a nameless country, one I know
I've never seen.

DEAR S—

Sometimes I think it's true that nothing's ours
to keep: no version of ourselves and
not the near-eruption of another heart
beating in sleep, so vigilant with dreaming
you can almost see it. Not the river,
the miles to the river, the angle of a body
as it leaps. Not the instant that it holds before falling
is the consequence of gravity. There is so much
we didn't really know before we lost it,
or turned left: our own bodies, those others,
the blue hill to the west. There's
a scientific principle that states we change
the heart of something just by looking
at it, so only what we've never seen
stays sturdy. The light is different
every time we turn our heads.
Our selves revisit us in altered shapes
but make a fist in the same way,
catch us in the same small, tender place
then open up their palms, say: *this
is a new country. This is already your home.*

Dear Maker,

Under my body's din,
       a hum that won't quiet,
I still hear what you've hidden
       in all the waves of sound:
each bead of pain
       that buries its head
like a blacklegged tick,
       intractable but mine
to nurse or lure with heat.
       Please, tell me
what it means that I've grown
       to love the steady sound
of so many kinds of caving in,
       buckling down, the way
a body gives itself away
       like a sullen bride or the runt
who couldn't latch? I know I'm just
       a hairline crack the music
leaves behind. I love
       the music, though I can't keep it.

Dear Maker,

Most stories lack magic: your lungs are too small,
 so you can't breathe, so you don't breathe,
so you die. Or you almost die, and then
 there's just a life, full of a lot of things that
have no place in myth: scalpel and stitches
 and too many dishes in the kitchen sink.
The problem is that not every story is a myth,
 is a sky where the body goes to star and back
again, is the body burning and burning and
 something else making it out.
I believe in all of you: the men who've held
 their hands around my bones and all the times
my muscles stretched to strings. My body is a violin
 somebody shaped in the first place, and the problem
is that every instrument has its own logic, fits the scale
 strangely if you hold it wrong. Mostly I'm not
making any music. I'm just living and now my lungs
 are the usual size and I breathe without effort;
everything else is a little more work. I am not alone
 in it. Watch, out the window the gulls are leaving
the ground and returning again.

RECOVERY

DEAR M—

I want to go back to before
I knew my body as shrapnel
and shred, a knife's serrated
edge, slick blade halving
the world as I cut through it.
It's impossible to go back,
but I want it anyway, endlessly,
the moment I'm a small and tender
beast, the fur of me still matted
by birth's strange coincidence.
I've been trying to learn
to be a gentler subject. I've been
trying to find a place where
someone puts their hands
around my waist and I don't split
them open with my own endless
splitting—where all my bones
stop hunting themselves
in the dark. Where I want to go
is lightless. I don't have to look
at the sharp animal I am:
the one who cleaves me open,
the one who seals me shut.

DEAR S—

I want to say I dreamed it, the returning,
but instead it is only the bodies of birds
with holes cut clean through their centers:
space featherless, fleshless, and eye-wide—
and a doe missing back legs, muscling
low through the undergrowth.
The hive of bees is wingless,
heavy as an anesthetic, radio-loud.
Everything's earthbound and nothing
has ever been whole. The better
beast is just a fiction, and maybe
it's better to know already I was
missing before I was born.

Dear M—

There's no going back,
no clearing to be found,
no curling ring of grass where
an animal, bedded down,
cries out and breaks me open
because she's calling back
to me, wherever I still wait,
from wherever it is we first
learned the body's another door
the world slams shut each time
we think to drag ourselves out
of the line of sight, beyond the scope
of whatever hand would yoke us
to each other, would have us
bent and humbled, poor machines,
poor beasts, whose tongues learn
first to cry and then to speak,
who can't go home, when where
we're from is already gone, already
burning down, graven inside us
like every ancient tree,
so we always know
who we belong to, where we
belong, where there's no going
back, or getting lost or found—

Dear S—

We are rewound: grow smaller and more animal,
come back unstitched, the hands inside of us rise up
into their sleeves, the knives are sheathed, the needle
punctures weave together perfect, blank, then absent.
Our tendons tighten down, our bones go back to bowing,
we curl, some hoof returns, the bodies that we know
revert to fictions from a place we didn't go.
             And where we are it's snowing,
and we're sheltered the way wild, loved things are when
they are new: a nest of winter grass, a little down,
some hollow where the weather strains to reach. Say that
we've never been afraid, we've never howled, we've never
been in pain. There's still a storm outside, there's still some
larger thing with teeth, there's still the day something will
nose us to get up and walk, then run, and when we can't
will leave without us, fearing yet another winter or a gun.

Dear M—

If we can't come stumbling
down the path that's never lit,
if we can't slip the wire fence
and if it rends our skin,
our hair, if we bleed, if we claw
the earth, if we don't call out
and nothing comes running, if we
rest awhile, if we wait and nothing
comes, M, will we stay tangled
in the wire, along the edge
of winter, if something gentle's
out of reach, will we stay and twist
the wire into shapes we know,
unshod hoof and bowed bone,
if we call them ours, if we make
such wire children and string
them up, if we rust, if our children
are wire stars above us, if they
are always out of reach, if we can't
twist free, if we bed down inside
ourselves, if our children swing
beyond us, if they don't resemble us—

Dear S—

If we're hooked in the fence,
if the ice on our hides names us
a thing for staying, but the children
we've contorted finally do twist free
of how we've strung them up—of both
the shapes we gave them and the ones
we wouldn't pass along—if they are
only a nurse's call light blinking
overhead, or the blood
we've loosed by chewing on our own
bad legs, or alluvium composed
of all the lither things that ran downhill
toward water. If we're left to work
the barbs out of the skin they bloomed in,
work out the differences in flesh,
and steel, and shade that nightfall has
false-miracled to bodies, cold—

Dear M—

Last night I dredged the river
again. I'd gone looking
for the children I left there,
the ones who catch like leaves
and twigs in the dam, the ones
I set down like little boats
and the ones I set down
like little stones. I'm beginning
to believe they were never
more than shadows, slipping
out of the recovery room while
I slept, leaving little notes
for me that disappeared as soon
as I thought to touch them.
        You said our eyes
can remake a thing, change
a shape by looking.
I don't want another thing
to lose its skin or come
undone. It's enough that
I can't remember the shapes
of the things I've loved
or the things I've made
in one body or another,
so I must make them up:
here is a heart-shaped hoof.
Here is a hoof-shaped heart.

DEAR S—

Last night I tried to sleep inside a blank
room. I made the bed a boat,
believed the smell of bleach was just
the water filling up with salt, just
gulls sounding outside the window, just
the tide and what it beaches, bone-bright,
on the cliffs. The ocean hunts itself at night
for all that has survived in the wrong place,
that has outlived its usefulness,
come loose, been lost, or fallen far
behind when other colonies have eased
right out to sea. It has a mechanism
for determining belonging, true as gravity
and all the quartz and lime and iron that
comprise the moon. I comb the beach
for shapes I recognize, and every night
my children don't wash up I think
there's still a chance for them,
and every night I don't find my own face
ripe for unmaking, I'm surprised.

DEAR MAKER,

My body keeps happening
        despite my insistence
otherwise: so I repeat myself:
        I'll tell you how: I start
at the beginning then end
        at the beginning: you were there
in all this, or are
        there: my mother who
carries me until winter: is there:
        was there and it is cold
when I arrived and the fact
        of me was small: and I arrive
again at the beginning
        and there we are: and here
keeps happening and when
        my mother looks at me
I'm sure I happen differently:
        each time I arrive: is a body
my body keeps:

Dear Maker,

It snows in this strange city.
       I'm bewildered by the white,
the way it makes one perfect
       creature of the place, one body
built up soundless overnight,
       then blown to pieces by the wind,
and how I barrel into it—my body
       as unsubtle here as anywhere.
I distrust the weather in my
       body—there's a sudden, shallow
warmth before tornadoes whistle
       damage down—before my body
had these seams there had to be
       a shattering I don't remember, you'd have
had to turn your face
       away from all the shards.

DEAR MAKER,

I'd say the problem isn't the story
       or that I'm in it, or that I resist the ways
I'm drawn. It's always been gravity and matter
       and the planet's relentless pull.
I resent the game. I don't want a seat at the table.
       I don't want a table either if it means everything
here is pinned down by its own weight. I'd say
       the problem is I haven't been sold on the ground
beneath me. Nobody told me the view
       is much better from space. When the planet becomes
just another raised fist in the distance, I don't mind.
       Though I'm poorly drawn, I still raise mine.

Dear Maker,

Listen, if I can't know
            what you first
whittled me out of
            I would like to see
the knife. The quick
            groove in an upper lip
is called a *philtrum,* like
            a blade slipped once,
caught just before
            the damage grew
too large to make
            the best of it, to fill
a body up with neat
            little canals and say
you *meant* to cut
            a river there. If I can't
know my body before
            it was riven, show me
your hands.
            Right now there's just
the ghost of how they
            turned around my body,
wrenched the whole thing
            toward another north.

OPERATING ROOM

DEAR M—

Today I forgot I was looking
for my own face, the shape
of something I should love.
I watched the leaves
gather around my feet,
their small dead selves lighter
now, unselved. Perhaps this is
part of it, this willingness
to forget the way the world
has touched our bodies sharply,
so we refill ourselves with
someone else: someone who
doesn't start every time
she hears a distant saw, who doesn't
feel her legs as deadwood, rot.
I want to be the kind of woman
who has one story and it's a good one,
and it starts like this: once,
I was in the dark woods.
          Here's the version I know
instead: nothing ever happens
once. The woods are everywhere.
The woods are rife with men
and saws and knives.
The trees, once, were alive.

Dear S—

Today I started walking where the trees were alive,
still stitched to their leaves, still humming, still houses
for musky warm and wild things who out-breathed all
the men and all their knives. And yes, the woods were dark,
but nothing ever happens once, and so they didn't stay
that way: the sun came up on the survivors
and there I was, somehow among their number, still
dragging the same legs, still finding buckshot caught
behind my tendons, braced for new machines
I might hear readying to work on all my flesh.
It turns out we can last a long time with our legs
bent, make it for miles crawling on our hands.
A callus forms, we grow a shell. In curling downward
it is easier to press our ears right to the ground,
hear that, beneath us both, where leaves and marrow
wear down and wear out, there's water running.
The woods, once, were something else.

DEAR M—

Would you say that once
the trees were bedded
down, the seeds of them
like us, caught in the dark,
that they broke themselves
open to know what lurked
inside, if they could last, if
they could turn in time
to press against the earth?
Would you say that birth
is the first hard frost
we somehow just survive,
and that, like us, the trees
learn spring isn't fast
or kind, but another way
the world takes stock
of what's allowed to stay?
A crowd of green masks
above our faces
closes in like trees.
What happens next
is never ours to say.

DEAR S—

If the trees know birth is just
another word for loss—that there's
a cost to shifting from seed
to sapling: all the shards
of what you were that don't
outlast the passage into light;
the way the weather breaks across
your back just when you learn its shape,
splits and scars the wood; how, if
you list in one direction there's a whole
side of the forest you'll never see—
then, god, I love that they do it anyway:
become themselves and stand there each
spring as it batters them to blooming, asks:
what would you weather just to call yourself alive?

Dear M—

Our faces are beyond recognition
and there are so many ways
I've failed to see myself
in the world, failed
to see the world in me,
though I've folded the woods
and the river into my arms, my chest,
so that I might be wrecked again,
so that I might be made
into another thing
the world forgets. I don't think
we'll ever recognize a place
as ours, as built for us, unless
it's one we make from the ashes
of the-next-best-thing, a nest
that's shaped by all the birds
before us. Even the raft
wasn't made for us, but of us,
our bodies unable to carry
themselves but made to carry
everything else. When I open
my hands, I'm never surprised
by the birds they turn into, how
quick they are to take a thing
apart to see what holds it up.
Take a little string, some gauze,
a piece of bark. Whatever it is
we carry into each clearing,
let's hold it up and squint
until it turns into a face we know,
a house we've loved, a wrecked
and empty nest, a place the birds
made for someone else,
then left.

DEAR S—

The birds our hands become
are the ones with holes cut
in their cores so you can see
right through them to the world
they're leaving toward: little globe
of cloud, or rusted brush, or green
held steady there between their bones while
they go on building and unbuilding
their homes from what was there already,
unspooling the string and tearing through
the air like they are not torn through,
like what's a wound was always
meant to be a window. I open my hands
and watch them work until they're out of sight.
       In one clearing, we settle down for a night
with what the birds have left behind,
in another, our hands make an aperture
somebody sees the sky through.

Dear M—

If what's a wound was always
meant to be a window, then say
my body's shot with light: say
it's me who looks, who
presses herself against the glassless
frame and waits for the riddled surfaces
to announce each version of the body
I've been, and the ones I think I'll become:
my mother's perfect face
that mine doesn't resemble, the idea
of a child I can't see, and so imagine
I might keep. Say it's me who
does the mapping: I name the river
and every gnarled tree, the places
that they reach: say I see
the whole of me blanch dry and white.
        Say home is a shard of bone I pull
from the riverbed, and say it's me
who cracks the earth to put it back.
The map is wrong. Someone else
shoots me through with light,
an X-ray a map I'm told is clear
and true, someone else cracks me
open too, names the earth, says
what shard comes out, what each
becomes, which piece goes back.

Dear S—

At the bottom of the riverbed
the ground is dry as all the shards
of bone we buried and unburied there.
I puzzle skeletons together from
the bleached scraps we wrenched loose,
trying to make an animal of what
they left us with when it was over.
I know I'm glowing from the artificial
stars they pumped us bright with,
that the rivers in my wrists are running
violet before they calcify. I'm leaking light.
I stain the things I touch. I lie down
in what is just a canyon now, and
watching from above, they use my
growing constellations to map out
the world they've made: pin down
the north, my waning water, what's
worth saving, how a good war spreads.

DEAR M—

What we leave down
in the canyon—the stain
of us—red on red,
hemoglobin on hematite,
the trace of us the one true
map we'll ever leave. Hidden
out of sight, a place only
forgotten animals tread, we're
pinned to slabs in outline
and sketch, the idea of us
a puzzle no one's yet seen
or read. Loosed
by bodies and their weight,
we start again, we take
another shape, we learn
our worth by learning
what we're not, like new
animals or children who,
finding themselves wingless, still
test the air and fall.

DEAR S—

Look, there, our dead
and heavy elements
are piled high beside
the silhouette of what
we were before—*look,*
there our prior selves
hush out like matches
once they've lit the pyre.
The light climbs high,
too far away from anybody's
home to be a flare. *Look,*
let's watch until the whole of it
cools first to smoke, then goes.
         I think we will be suited for it:
being legless, weightless,
wingless, leaping off—

DEAR MAKER,

Even if it's true that my body's
        just a transitory letter, a note
you sent, a piece of paper
        covered with your writing,
I'd like to know what it is
        you meant, if I could mean
something other than what
        all lost letters mean: a gesture
no one sees, what all good
        storms erase. I'd like to be
read out loud in a voice
        that's all my own. I'd
like to be read with gusto.
        Where your writing trails off,
I'd like to see my failed
        hand start: *Dear Maker, Dear
Other, Dear Lost One, Dear
        Me*—do you see them coming?
Can you make them out,
        those clouds shaped like envelopes,
the way they fold themselves
        to keep their contents close?

Dear Maker,

Look at the marble table, the cleaver, and the stars
        they built to watch the butchering. The human
constellations cut into the ceiling there,
        hosts of older gods and men of science lined
shoulder to shoulder, sharp as buzzards, on the walls.
        I'm half a world away from the country I was born in
and this is not a church, but Maker, *look,* here is what
        I believe in. All those years ago they butterflied
a body just to put their hands inside, learn
        ligament, lymph node, liver, and lung, how one
piece dictates another, how a creature runs.
        One man bent over another and forgot himself,
thought *look, what's done can be undone and redone better,*
        took a chisel, and a saw, and some string to the body,
pared away error, practiced what would one day
        make me: how to see the body as a country you can
section and redraw without a sacrifice. *Look,* here
        your face clouds over, here a whole new kind
of grief is borne out under whittled stars.

PRE-OP HOLDING ROOM

DEAR M—

If you're right, if everything
glows bright, stains at our touch,
our artificial light, then
we've made it somewhere
past the map's rough edge,
where bodies move without
a thought for what they trail
behind, where the trail we leave
can always be retraced yet no
one's tracked us here, where
we move beyond the body's edges
and the names we drag, where
the only ones who make it
through the underbrush must
navigate by lantern light and
dust, and self-made shadows
stretching out like guides
who lead us deeper into night,
so long as we carry lightboxes
in our mouths, our eyes,
so long as we burn beyond
ourselves like stars, spread
ourselves thin and far, for all
the years and miles we've yet
to see or make or know,
the miles of road, the stones
a trail we leave behind us, glinting
bright and surgical as eyes
that watch us from below.

DEAR S—

From our mouths the dye is seeping, too:
the artificial stars have come alive, have grown
wings to beat against the lightbox glass
until it breaks and they come spilling out and swarm
then scatter overhead, shattered by all the shadow selves
who found us in the canyon, pulled us burning,
here, beyond the map's margin.
        The whole place glows and pulses now, the way
the dark does when it's deep as water. The shadow
selves forge on. We track them like a pulse. S, you're right,
wherever we are now is somewhere we've never
been. Maybe there is a lake. Maybe a mountain
range laid out along the bottom. Maybe we step out
of our bodies like long coats burned mostly off, maybe
the eyes that watch us from below are better stars.

Dear M—

For once I'm glad to be led
to water and asked to drink, to be
untracked, unfollowed,
to let the light in our mouths beat
against every rough surface, until
we know every given thing by its white
marrow, until the only world we know
is a raised root system, a garden
of twined scars that threads our skin
like the river we can't outrun.
Let's set them loose from their cages, the birds,
set the songs loose from their throats,
and crack open our own to welcome
what may come: another way to speak,
a little song, an elegy for all the selves
we couldn't save, or wouldn't.

Dear S—

If our throats crack open
as we reach the bank
and they're the last whole
parts of us to yield a river
when we're butterflied,
if what pours out
is everything we've carried
on the current all our lives:
stones and steel, scraps
of fabricated sky, the silt from
every drug that didn't dissolve
then *become* us. If it
comes loose and rushes
for the door we've shaped
and leaves us with a small, blank
room to do our claiming in,
Will we even recognize
the sounds we make, know
that their echoing means
grief or *knife* or *sister,*
want, arrival, or our names?

Dear M—

For want of arrival, a clear
syllable that opens across
the room or the field
between us, give me
instead the earth and silt
our names become
with each labored
step, the dust of our
names inconvenient and
undeniable in the light,
the way they collect in the corner
of a stranger's room, all
the ways they're uttered,
the ways we heed: give me
crooked bird, wildflower, chokeweed.
       Give me a picture of two girls
crouched low, a list of things
belonging to them: what
grows along the ground.
What turns back on itself
as it goes.

Dear S—

Chokeweed: small white flowers like bells
that crawl over all the canyons
and trees, every bed the girls
once occupied, all the bent bodies
bent again until they'd cease
hunting themselves, cease curling in.
Until they'd heed. Let's make more
of it, let's spur it on, let's water it until
the girls sit down in the dust,
until it climbs their folded legs and up
then down their throats, until we cannot tell
them from the ground, from hills, muscle
from flower, from ringing, tell whatever
belonged to them from the field, tell
the field from wherever we are now.

DEAR M—

This is how we thrive,
when we spread across
the field, the sky, when
we're cut down to root
and stub, the unlikely weed
we try to pull but then
become, and everything
is ours to take, surround
with vines, and everything
that's left in the dirt
or left behind is ours to lift,
is us, new bodies we make
of bone, shards, hurt,
of loss, twine, trash,
and so much grime
the sheen of us runs gold,
runs dry until we split
our piecemeal skins, and what
we've taken spills at our feet,
spills before our eyes, and look
how we lift ourselves
from dirt—

Dear S—

In this elsewhere
where we've landed,
bloomed beyond
our stitches—
on this other
shore, where we
have disembarked
our bodies like the boats
they are, and watched
the shine that rises from
the drying wood and called
it ours for the last time—
in this place beyond
the maps they made,
the logbooks where
we read that we should
know ourselves as
error, element,
and remedy—
here, will we watch
the started-selves
we spilled out on
the earth take root,
lift from the dirt,
stretch out in their
new skin, test
bone and sudden
boundedness? Will
we watch them raise
a hand to touch
their brand new mouths,
their shoulder blades,
their shins and spines
and easy joints and know
themselves as they have
always been? Will
we call it grief or
something brighter just
to watch them go?

Dear M—

I'd like to think as we lift
ourselves to go, in this newness
we leave it all behind—a grave, a name,
a birthday, a face—in favor
of what we know is ours
to make, this record
of our speech, our grief,
that we'll turn away from
all the doors that wouldn't
open, every collapsed bridge,
and hail instead the space
between us, shapeless and
endless as it is, though
we hold it between us
just the same.

Dear S—

In the field between us:
a softer season—summer
maybe, early, when the grass
has grown waist high but not
yet yellowed from the heat—
in the rubble of a fallen bridge,
in all the weeds and dandelion
down, we've made a place we
didn't need to call a house to feel
at home. And on the ridge ahead
we see small, dark creatures
rising in the air: birds, bats, loosed
barn owls, our not-yet-children
testing out the world before they
find us where we've settled
for a while, looked toward the sky.

Dear—

We wade the switchgrass to see what ripples,
                    to see what rises from the grass, waist-high, to hear what sings

in the wake of what we aren't: not winged or weightless not bound
                    by the light from the radio tower, not the last of the ice

then threshed, spent by a hard wind turning north
                    the living things extend their necks into the air, bear all that wanting

turning wild with our wildness: call it kinship for distance
                    call it knowing where we find ourselves

that we cross or braid or bear, between us the living field
                    carrying the homes we whittled when we had to

breathing under us, a place where water
                    a place where all the burning things blaze out at once

and more water carries away what's left: the dead, the bent, the breath,
                    the ash, the shadows all still straining some to look like what they were

and what we could have been: a bright and endless music, an animal set out
                    sturdy and straight, seeing itself repeated out into the distance as it goes.